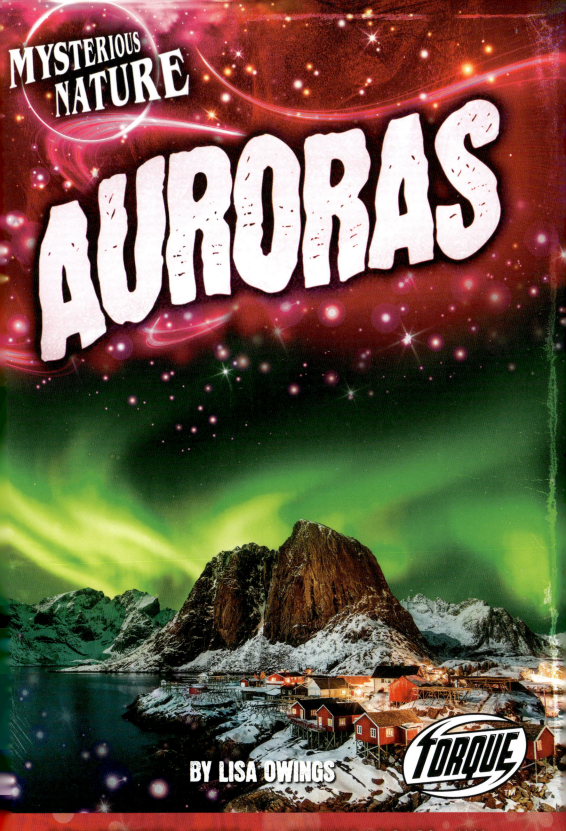

Torque brims with excitement perfect for thrill-seekers of all kinds. Discover daring survival skills, explore uncharted worlds, and marvel at mighty engines and extreme sports. In *Torque* books, anything can happen. Are you ready?

This edition first published in 2025 by Bellwether Media, Inc.

No part of this publication may be reproduced in whole or in part without written permission of the publisher. For information regarding permission, write to Bellwether Media, Inc., Attention: Permissions Department, 6012 Blue Circle Drive, Minnetonka, MN 55343.

Library of Congress Cataloging-in-Publication Data

LC record for Auroras available at: https://lccn.loc.gov/2024009435

Text copyright © 2025 by Bellwether Media, Inc. TORQUE and associated logos are trademarks and/or registered trademarks of Bellwether Media, Inc. Bellwether Media is a division of Chrysalis Education Group.

Editor: Rebecca Sabelko   Designer: Josh Brink

Printed in the United States of America, North Mankato, MN.

TABLE OF CONTENTS

LIGHTS IN THE SKY	4
WHAT ARE AURORAS?	6
FOX TAILS AND FLAMES	10
THE SOLAR WIND	16
GLOSSARY	22
TO LEARN MORE	23
INDEX	24

Lights in the Sky

It is cold and clear. People gather outside as the Sun goes down. It is the perfect night to see an aurora!

Names North to South

Auroras over the North Pole are called the northern lights, or aurora borealis. People near the South Pole may see the southern lights, or aurora australis.

Soon, a green glow spreads across the sky. The glow turns into dancing lights. They curl like ribbons. They shift into cloud shapes. Everyone forgets the cold as they watch in amazement!

What Are Auroras?

Auroras are natural light displays in the sky. They can only be seen at night. Auroras are most often green. Red, blue, and other colors can appear, too.

The lights can form bands, swirls, and rays. They can change shape quickly or hardly at all. At times, they are just a soft glow. Scientists have recorded eerie whistling and crackling sounds during strong auroras.

Otherwordly Auroras

Jupiter

Saturn

Uranus

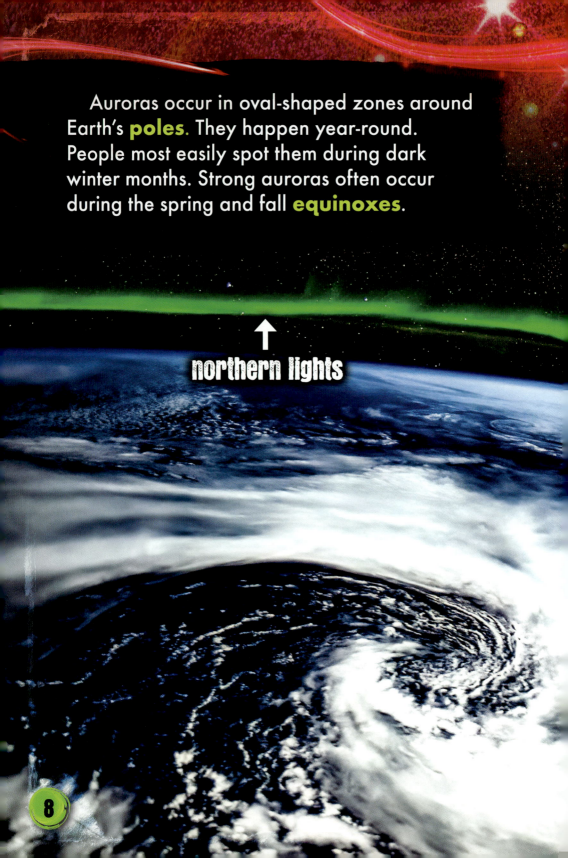

Auroras occur in oval-shaped zones around Earth's **poles**. They happen year-round. People most easily spot them during dark winter months. Strong auroras often occur during the spring and fall **equinoxes**.

↑
northern lights

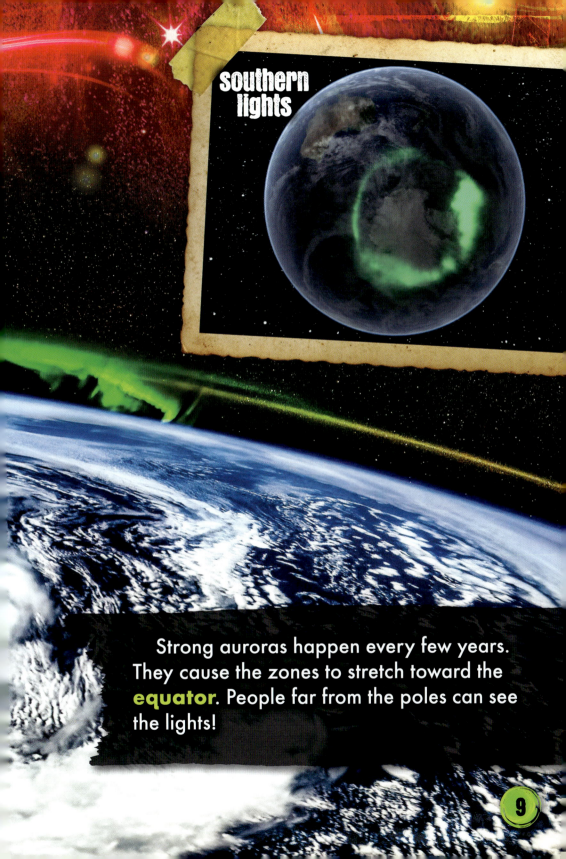

southern lights

Strong auroras happen every few years. They cause the zones to stretch toward the **equator**. People far from the poles can see the lights!

Fox Tails and Flames

Humans have watched auroras in wonder for thousands of years. Some welcomed the lights. People in Finland thought auroras looked like sparks flying from foxes' tails. Fishers from Sweden believed the lights danced off schools of herring.

The Maori believed auroras were lights from the campfires of their **ancestors**. Other **cultures** thought auroras would cause **disasters**.

Souls of the Sámi

 Who believes it? Sámi people of Scandinavia

 What do they believe? The lights are the souls of the dead who carry the living away.

ANCIENT AURORAS
People made cave paintings of auroras. One is at least 30,000 years old!

In 1619, Galileo Galilei named auroras after the Roman goddess of dawn. He and other scientists tried to understand the lights. By the 1700s, most scientists believed auroras were light **reflected** from the Sun.

Edmond Halley saw an aurora in 1716. This led him to a new idea. Halley was the first to suggest that auroras had to do with Earth's **magnetic field**.

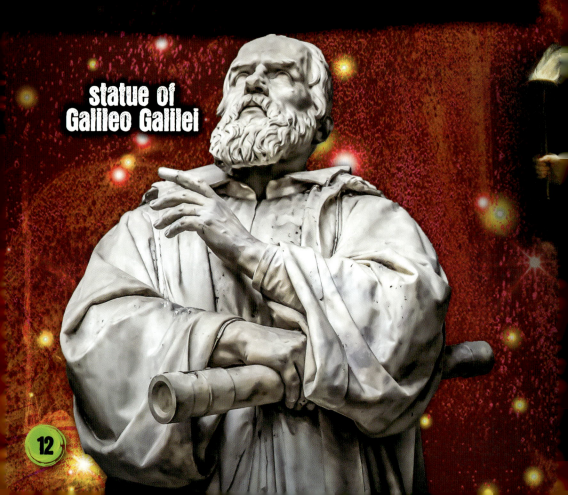

statue of Galileo Galilei

Edmond Halley

painting of Aurora, the Roman goddess of dawn

THE COMING OF DAWN

Ancient Romans believed the goddess Aurora rode across the sky each night. She announced the coming of the new day.

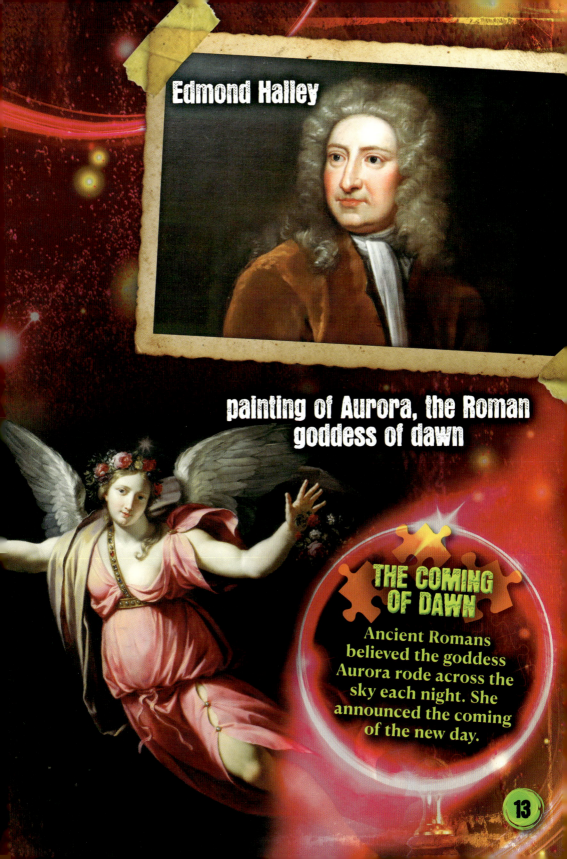

Richard Carrington witnessed a bright flash from the Sun followed by strong auroras in 1859. He believed the two events were connected.

The Carrington Event

 When was it spotted? September 1 to 2, 1859

 Where was it spotted? Around the world

 Who studied it? Richard Carrington in Redhill, Surrey, England

 What did they see? Carrington saw a bright flash from the Sun followed by auroras that were seen across much of the globe.

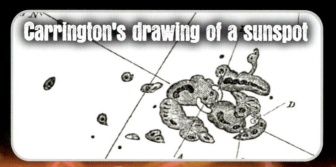
Carrington's drawing of a sunspot

HOW HIGH?
Henry Cavendish was the first to take measurements of an aurora. In 1790, he found that auroras began about 60 miles (97 kilometers) above Earth.

Kristian Birkeland

Kristian Birkeland studied Carrington's idea in the early 1900s. He built **models** that showed how **particles** from the Sun could light up Earth's poles. Few believed him. But others proved him right years later.

The Solar Wind

Auroras occur when charged particles from the Sun meet gases in Earth's **atmosphere**. Particles charged with **energy** leave the Sun. They speed toward Earth. This is called the **solar wind**.

The Science of Auroras

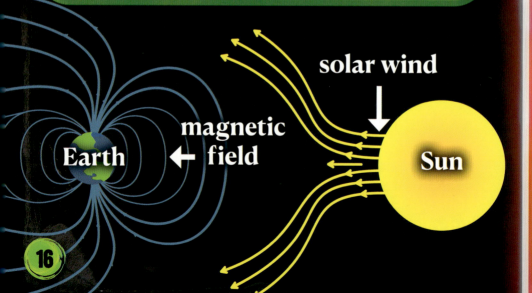

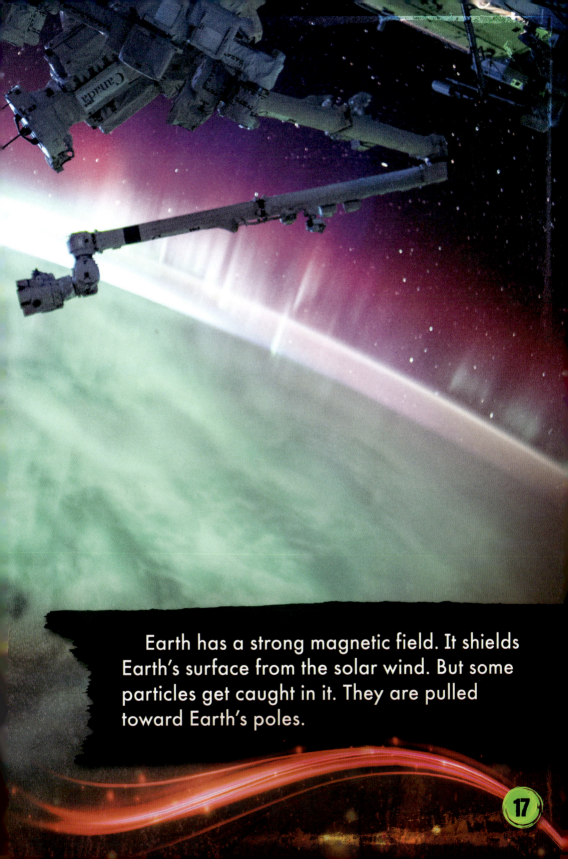

Earth has a strong magnetic field. It shields Earth's surface from the solar wind. But some particles get caught in it. They are pulled toward Earth's poles.

The solar wind particles crash into gases in Earth's atmosphere. All these tiny crashes release energy. The energy appears as the lights of an aurora.

Different gases create different colors. Green or red occur when the solar wind hits oxygen. Hydrogen glows blue or purple. Nitrogen causes pink.

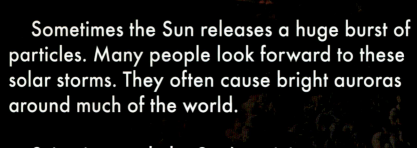

Sometimes the Sun releases a huge burst of particles. Many people look forward to these solar storms. They often cause bright auroras around much of the world.

Scientists track the Sun's activity. They **predict** when and where auroras will happen. They let people know when auroras might swirl across the night sky!

GLOSSARY

ancestors—relatives from long ago

atmosphere—the layers of gases around a planet

cultures—societies that hold the same beliefs, arts, and ways of life

disasters—sudden events that cause great damage or loss

energy—power from the Sun that helps create auroras

equator—the imaginary line that divides Earth into northern and southern halves

equinoxes—the two times of year when the Sun passes directly over the equator

magnetic field—the area around a magnetic object that is affected by its force

models—small, 3D versions of objects; models are built to show what something looks like or how it works.

particles—tiny bits of matter; matter is materials that form objects and take up space.

poles—the northernmost and southernmost points of Earth

predict—to use information to guess what may happen

reflected—bounced off of a surface and bent in another direction

solar wind—a stream of charged particles from the Sun

TO LEARN MORE

AT THE LIBRARY

Kingston, Seth. *Northern Lights*. New York, N.Y.: PowerKids Press, 2021.

Morey, Allan. *Solar Storm*. Minneapolis, Minn.: Bellwether Media, 2020.

Thacher, Meg. *Sky Gazing: A Guide to the Moon, Sun, Planets, Stars, Eclipses, Constellations*. North Adams, Mass.: Storey Publishing, 2020.

ON THE WEB

FACTSURFER

Factsurfer.com gives you a safe, fun way to find more information.

1. Go to www.factsurfer.com

2. Enter "auroras" into the search box and click 🔍.

3. Select your book cover to see a list of related content.

INDEX

ancient Romans, 13
atmosphere, 16, 18
Birkeland, Kristian, 15
Carrington Event, 14
Carrington, Richard, 14, 15
Cavendish, Henry, 15
cave paintings, 11
colors, 5, 6, 19
cultures, 10
Earth, 8, 12, 15, 16, 17, 18
energy, 16, 18
equator, 9
equinoxes, 8
explanation, 16, 17, 18, 19, 20
Finland, 10
Galilei, Galileo, 12
gases, 16, 18, 19
Halley, Edmond, 12, 13
history, 10, 11, 12, 13, 14, 15

magnetic field, 12, 17
Maori, 10
models, 15
names, 4, 12
night, 4, 6, 13, 20
otherworldly auroras, 7
particles, 15, 16, 17, 18, 20
poles, 4, 8, 9, 15, 17
Sámi, 11
science of auroras, 16
seasons, 8
shapes, 5, 7
solar storms, 20
solar wind, 16, 17, 18, 19
sounds, 7
Sun, 4, 12, 14, 15, 16, 20
Sweden, 10
zones, 8, 9

The images in this book are reproduced through the courtesy of: Piotr Krzeslak, front cover (hero); lightpix, pp. 2-3, 22-24; Parilov, pp. 4-5; Mike-Hubert.com, pp. 6-7; Worldspec/NASA/ Alamy, p. 7 (Saturn); NASA, ESA, and J. Nichols (University of Leicester)/ Wiki Commons, p. 7 (Jupiter); NASA, ESA, and L.Lamy (Observatory of Paris, CNRS, CNES)/ Wiki Commons, p. 7 (Uranus); SpaceEnhanced/ Alamy, pp. 8-9; NG Images/ Alamy, p. 9 (southern lights); Bildagentur Zoonar GmbH, pp. 10-11; Granbergs Nya Aktiebolag/ Wiki Commons, p. 11 (Sámi people); Ilia Baksheev, p. 12 (statue of Galileo Galilei); Fine Art Images/Heritage Images/ Alamy, pp. 12-13 (goddess of dawn); Uwe Deffner/ Alamy, p. 13 (Edmond Halley); The Picture Art Collection/ Alamy, p. 14; FLHC MADB1/ Alamy, pp. 14-15; VectorMine, p. 16 (science of auroras); Nasa/UPI/ Alamy, pp. 16-17; Gareth Davies/ Alamy, pp. 18-19; muratart, p. 19; Tsuguliev, pp. 20-21.